THE RAVEN
AND THE SUN

Poems and Stories
by Boria Sax

THE POET'S PRESS

Also available as a PDF E-Book.

This is the 184th publication of
THE POET'S PRESS
2209 Murray Avenue #3
Pittsburgh, PA 15217

www.poetspress.org

CONTENTS

STORIES

THE RAVEN
AND THE SUN

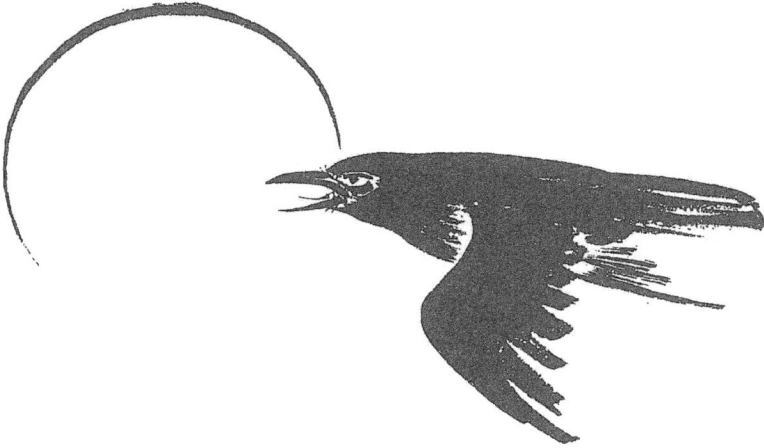

To all my friends —

TELLING NATURE'S STORY:
A MANIFESTO

Stories are not confined to human beings. Every animal, plant, stream, or mountain has a story.

Scholars are storytellers, who must now help to tell the story of humankind, of the earth, of the cosmos, of the troubled marriage between Mother Nature and Father Culture. These should be told in a language that can convey both intellectual nuance and emotional intensity, together with high drama, humor, pathos, adventure, and romance.

To tell the story of a tree or a butterfly is to grant it what is sometimes called "personhood."

The majestic protocols of scholarship add authority and dignity, but they should not become the reason why we write. Documentation should enhance, not overwhelm, the story. Noting special cases should add interest and variety, and qualifications should enhance suppleness. But the accumulated mass of detail must not distract us from the line of narrative.

Language is not confined to human beings, though our language is like no other. There is also the dance of a bee, the changing colors of an octopus, the architecture of a bower bird, and the howling of a wolf. There is the language of the genetic code, with which strands of DNA speak to an embryo, or of plants as they bend and turn to share the sun.

The laws of physics are the grammar of a language in which the stars and galaxies communicate with one another. Are we speaking metaphorically? Sure. But that is how our language works.

Computers also have languages. We may use their languages when we communicate with them, but human beings do not use computer languages to talk with one another. We also do not habitually dance like bees nor bark like crows. That is because our language is not simply an accessory. It is a basic part of what we are.

Humankind does not simply *have* a story; humankind *is* a story. While that story is still told, humanity will live. When the story ends, humankind will be no more. Our DNA, if it survives, will be one more monument alongside Stonehenge and the paintings in Lascaux.

< 9 >

What is Nature? All things that we are not. It is our beloved partner and adversary. Nature is a spider, gazing at a boy as she turns, with each of eight arachnid eyes, hanging from a filament catches the sun momentarily and then seems to disappear.

Didn't Aristotle point out that things are opposite only through the qualities they share? The story of nature is our story, just as the reflection in a pond is our image, in reverse. Without Nature we could not live; in fact we could not even die.

< 10 >

POEMS

WITHIN AN APPLE SEED

"Inside your walls
Are generations of trees,
A vast horizon
And apples enough to last
Until the end of time,
So, surely, there is room
For me as well...

Let me in!"
I call, yet nobody
Answers, for those in the seed
Are resting underneath
A fragrant bough.
One thinks, "Is that a squirrel
In the leaves?"

< 13 >

THE ENDLESS PARADE OF WOMEN

A young girl, her books tucked beneath her arm, hurrying
   to school as her lips form secret words.
A purity shining from her face the ways trees, roads and
   even darkness shine at night after the rain —
A kind of loneliness, of joy, of curiosity, all slightly different
   from a man's.
An old woman, her arms grown frail and her gestures sure
   and her face become unique for all the lines.
The endless parade of women, descending a stairway,
   resting in a park, strolling along the street.
The rhythm of their footsteps, the way their voices fall,
   the signs and the glances they exchange.
A little boy, slightly awkward, very much amazed,
   in a room filled with many women —
To watch discreetly this one's eyebrow being raised,
   that one's finger playing with a pen or perhaps
   the special curve of this one's knee.
The things no man can ever know, the smile he cannot
   imitate, the thoughts he cannot imagine and the words
   he could never say.
Their strangeness and their beauty — the first snow
   of the year — glittering round him in the sunshine
   on every side.

< 14 >

WHAT IS IT LIKE. . . ?

What is it like to have a woman's face?
A woman's body? With a woman's hand?
No man can step into a woman's place.
I certainly will never understand.

What is it like to have a woman's eyes?
I wonder, would a rainbow look the same?
Is it one fabric but with other dyes?
Is it one picture with another frame?

I asked a woman once. She would not say.
She only laughed and touched me on the arm,
Then looked about her in a secret way.
"At least," I thought, "I've not done any harm."

A woman brings such power to her touch.
How could a man be trusted with so much?

< 15 >

OLD MILK BOTTLE

The sides are heavy like an earthen pot
Of long ago, but they are made of glass.
The milkman, coming with the morning light,
Delivered them to houses on the block,
Filled up with milk, and took the empty ones.
The families left notes yet seldom saw his face.
I never did, for little boys sleep long.
I sometimes heard his footsteps and the clang
Of bottles rattling in their metal frames,
And I imagined him, dressed all in white
Like the early morning when he came.

< 16 >

OBJECTS

Our universe is the abandoned room
Of a child, filled with dresses, books, and dolls,
Things she outgrew but never threw away —
Broken mirrors, combs with missing teeth,
Chess pieces, buttons, strands of faded yarn. . .

Do objects meditate? Do objects think?
We sometimes love them? Is that love returned?
Photographs, comic books, a lock of hair,
A bird's nest, a puppet with no strings,
A smashed computer, and a rubber ball,
Lost on a rafter, nearly out of sight.
Bits of glitter, enormous clouds of dust...
Waiting for their mistress to return.

< 17 >

THE PHYSICIST

Even in matter, in barren earth and stone, there is something
    straining to find a voice, to walk upright, to love.
He will come home at midnight to stare at a page full
    of numbers and envy their immortality.
Outside the darkness heaves and sighs, to circle around
    his house and frighten him.

Like something in a microscope, they move — the plates
    and graphs, the arrows, broken lines, and winding arcs.
Is there a rip in the fabric of reality? The sky could become
    unraveled, the stars fall in a sparkling heap,
Like the curtain going down after a carnival, to be raised
    as another show begins.

He wonders if those fragments of the night
Might rise from the white ocean of his page
Like the first men appearing on this earth.

< 18 >

COCOON

If a caterpillar becomes a butterfly,
What might a snake become?
A griffin, that unfolds a single wing
And stretches out a claw
As, gradually, it awakens
To emerge from a cocoon.

< 19 >

A BLEEDING STAR

One line for the horizon,
The black scar
A child slashed across the page.
A bleeding star
Had risen from the wound.
He drew himself, then threw
The sheet away.

Globes of rain
Soaked fibers of the page
To etch a pattern
Delicate as frost, and wind
Raised, whirled, and flung down
That fragile world;
A woman picked it up and took it home.

The boy was soon a man, and found the page.
The crayon sun asked,
"Can I shine again?"
The crayon boy asked,
"What have I become?"
The man said nothing, but his face said all.
He tossed the drawing into a fire.

< 20 >

THE ROOM

I sit in my room. If a friend asked me to describe it, I would say, "just a room." I would scarcely believe that he did not know it, that he did not know the color of the walls, the arrangement of the chairs, the pictures on the wall. That comes with familiarity, yet, when I move, the room becomes strange and exotic, more so with every piece of furniture that is taken away. Finally, it stands empty, ready to absorb another destiny, like a child who is leaving home. Yet it is I who am leaving. How many rooms I have left behind! I think of all the rooms where I have ever slept, from childhood until now. I line them up like compartments in a train. I put them all into a vast hotel. I am the night watchman, looking through each one.

< 21 >

LOSS

Time to bind up another plastic bag
Of soggy newspapers, tin cans, and coffee grounds,
And every single item signifies
At least another minute of my life.
But now I'll haul that sack into the yard,
And strangers will toss it in a dump.

Suppose all things that I have thrown away
Throughout my life were piled up.
There would be one more mountain on the globe
For vines to climb, and, when it turned to dirt,
A village might be built along its base.

< 22 >

WEEHAWKEN, NJ

I view Manhattan from across the Hudson
And 42nd Street is like a Christmas tree,
Wide at the base, but leading
Smoothly, gracefully, up to a point.
But globes of light are really porno shops
And movie houses, with garish neon signs.

The pimps, whores, businessmen, tourists,
Cops, pushers, and runaways and all the rest
Are tiny dots of color, blending
In brilliant golden tones,
Changing, so very slowly, as the sky
Grows darker and then light again.
"Beautiful," you say, yet I'm afraid,
For what we see is ruin and decay.
If these things can be beautiful,
How can we trust beauty any more?

ROSES IN A FOREST

A woman took some plots of earth
About six inches wide, declaring
These enchanted circles
To represent the woods inside her home.
In these she placed some bulbs
And nurtured them
Like children, bestowing food
And water till they grew.
She left, spurred on by dreams
Or poverty. A lilac tapped
Against the window sill
And entered, embraced by the rose.

< 24 >

THE DOE

A doe had lost her shyness and approached
An open field by the cottage where I stayed.
She looked at me, and then she turned away,
Moving and turning in a changing cloud
Of fireflies, around her like the wind,
As though she were a mythic beast that priests
Or mariners found pictured in the stars
Against the background of the Milky Way.

She stamped twice on the ground then strolled
In my direction, nibbling at the grass.
I thought: Perhaps if I approach the doe
Slowly enough and with no sudden noise,
I might talk to her and touch her side
Before she bounded off into the woods.
Then, on reflection, it seemed better far
That deer not lose their shyness or their fear
Of men and women. People carry guns.
That doe was far too friendly or too bold.

< 25 >

CROW STORIES

Do animals tell stories to one another? If so, are they tragic stories or funny stories? Are they short stories with lessons, like the fables of Aesop? Are they stories that never end, like those told to the Sultan by Scheherazade?

The other day, I saw a crow sitting quietly on a branch, when another flew up to it, cawing frantically. The first crow remained mute and motionless, while the other, growing louder and more excited, circled her head a few times.

The second crow then dived downward past the first, just barely missing her, but crow number one appeared completely unperturbed.

This happened another time, and then a third, when at last the two flew off together.

< 26 >

THE MAN WHO DISCOVERED FIRE

As sparks first leapt out of a battered stone,
The shaman could foresee a time of swords,
Then bombs and battleships, and so he made
A limestone edifice, sacred to the gods,
He thought might shield him. He called it "home,"
His refuge, fort, and prison all in one.
Inside his hearth, he would see Babylons
Like Paris, Timbuktu, and Samarkand.

I am that man! This city is my dream.
When traffic lights turn green, I hear the trees,
Which moan as they're cut down, and as I walk
The New York boulevards, an echo cries,
"This street will be a forest once again."

< 27 >

THE JAYS, THE HAWK, AND THE WARRIOR

Yesterday, I watched two blue jays mobbing a hawk, which was perched on a dead branch beside a pond. The hawk had, no doubt, invaded their territory, and they probably had a nest of chicks nearby. The jays circled the raptor's head and even dived, so recklessly, beneath her beak, as though daring her to pounce, whistling harshly the entire time. The hawk remained completely motionless, as though it would not deign to even acknowledge the presence of such rabble. At last, though, she wearily raised her shoulders, slowly spread her wings, flapped a few times, then sped away.

After the hawk had left, the jays were also nowhere to be seen, yet I glimpsed one a minute later passing quietly overhead. This was a drama of life and death, yet, for the birds, a thing that might happen every day. Had the jays been frightened? No doubt, but not with the overpowering terror that fills the human soul. The dread was softened by an element of play.

Human warriors, by contrast, wear costumes replete with plumes, gold braid, and gleaming pins. They parade in splendor, wave swords and recite verse, all in a desperate effort to convince themselves and others that war is a game.

< 28 >

4000 B.C.

The dead surround them like shy animals,
But they are certain they can live forever.
Whatever happens, they must find a way.

The next thousand years shall pass quickly.
The stones shall keep their oath of silence.
The trees shall go on talking in their sleep.

Men shall spend their days dragging blocks of stone
And their nights in conversation with the dead.
They shall polish daggers behind the city wall.

They shall carve diamonds and drive chariots.
They shall try to imagine that muscular hand
That lifted mountains and arranged the stars.

< 29 >

THAT VILLAGE

Somewhere, there is a village
Surrounded by modest fields and woods,
So ordinary, so mundane,
That, though known, it remains unnoticed.
A unicorn munches on the foliage
Along the fence of somebody's home,
But the unicorn appears natural,
Ordinary, and even a bit dull.
Nobody thinks: "That is a unicorn!"
Nobody calls the zoo or the police.
A griffin lands on a steeple.
Nobody points or stares.

And where is this village?
Not far away at all.
You may have stopped there once
To drink your morning coffee
And read *The New York Times*.

< 30 >

WIND

In distant trees, I see the approaching gale.
It seems the wind might blow the moon from its orbit,
To be lost like a spark among the clouds.
It seems the wind might bend rays of light
From the sun, like streamers at a fair.
It seems the wind might twist time and space —
To send planets floating through the void.
And yet, should I fear the wind?
The leaves cling so tightly to their branches,
Hardly a one is lost.

< 31 >

THE WOODSMAN, DEATH

For a man, there is "death."
For a tree, we need another word,
For that flash of extinction
May last until an infant
Tells a story to his granddaughter
And is buried by his son.

What is death? What is life?
Before the soul has departed from a tree,
Worms nibble at the corpse,
And squirrels leap through the outstretched hands.
Bees make their home inside the ribs,
And sparrows nest in the skull.

The tree welcomes such travelers
Without regret or pain.
Though appendages may crack
Burst, crumble, and decay,
The spirit can yet ordain
A last, irrevocably final, leaf,
A message for the soil...

< 32 >

NIGHT

A spider has stretched
Her web across a ditch.
A few changing strands
Catch the light as I walk along
Like strings of a lute
Played by the moon.

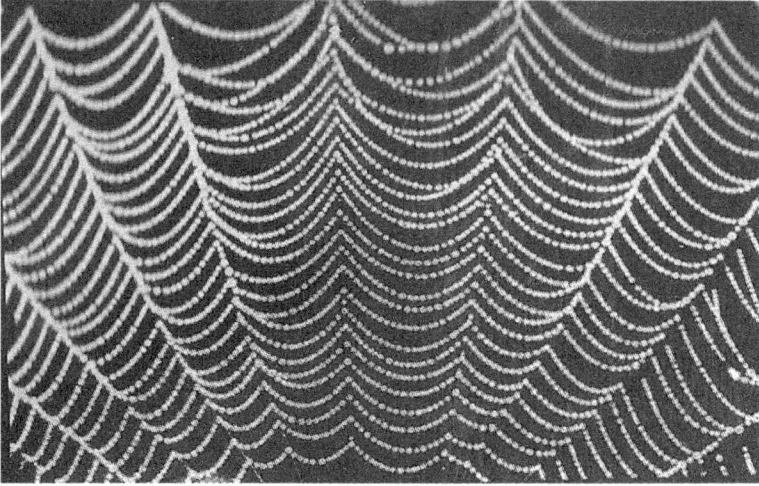

< 33 >

OLD TALES

The earth has gone on turning in her sleep,
Through battles, hurricanes, and atom bombs.
Our revolutions have not changed much....

Let me hear stories of great love and anger,
Of sorrow, magnificent as stars over Babylon
Or dinosaurs on a volcanic plain.

< 34 >

GRANDMOTHER, 1983

Four miles to the nearest shop or town,
A single mile to the nearest farm,
Grandmother owns a ragged plot of land
And no-one knows exactly where it starts.
There was barbed wire there when I was small,
Behind it was a field of geese and cows.
The wire has disappeared. The field is overgrown.
A few trees are cut down, but yet the cottages
Have only lost some paint in all those years.
They needed a coat then — and need it still.

She was as old as anyone could be,
Or so we thought, but she is older now.
Her husband, son and daughter all are dead.
One grandchild has died. The rest are grown.
A neighbor painted her, a gnarled branch in hand,
The long white hair bound up upon her head,
The trees above her, taller every year.
She walked the path she's walked so many times.
When she too dies, then all of this will change;
Weeds overwhelm the paths her feet have worn.

A Russian village was her only home.
She never felt at ease upon these shores
With autos, bank accounts, insurance, bills,
Policemen shouting, planes, and neon signs
(No more am I, but somehow I get by).
She always shouted on the telephone.
It may be she still plots against the Tsar,
But he is dead. And she will die as well.
The rooms that she has lived in fifty years
Will fall into decay or else be sold.

< 35 >

BESTIARY

The elephant:
An asteroid
That struck earth
And walked.

The moth:
An autumn leaf
Flying
Without a breeze.

Dolphins:
Waves
That did not vanish
Into the sea.

A jellyfish:
The dream
Of a mariner
Who drowned.

The lion:
A field of sun
Curled up
For the night.

Each minnow:
A pebble
The ocean caressed
And coaxed to life.

< 36 >

THE JELLYFISH

The water is her breath, her food,
Her thought, and minnows swim
Among her tentacles,
Like ladies in a dream.

The jellyfish, pulsing rhythmically
With water in every fold,
From every wave or current,
Believes she is the ocean.

What does the ocean think?
Might he say, "I am a jellyfish,"
If oceans spoke, and not just
Through the wind?

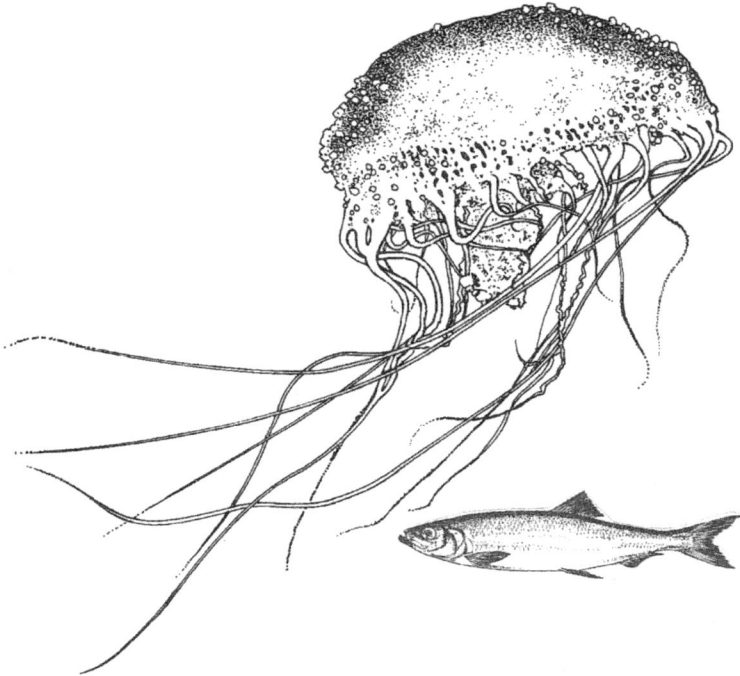

< 37 >

SOMETHING ABOUT THE WEATHER

Overcome by rage, a waiter
Shatters his tray against the grass.
It is something about the weather,
the way shadows fall.
Something is wrong. Even pigeons
Flutter nervously about.

It is a day for suicide,
For revelations, for secret joy.
An undertaker realizes
He has been talking to the dead,
And it occurs to a nurse —
She is no longer moved by pain.

A banker stares out his window,
To dream of ecstasies known only to the poor.
There is the moan of the refrigerator,
The painful grinding of the clock.
The river moves as if it were alive.
The thunder rises slowly from the ground

< 38 >

UMKRAUT GEHT NICHT KAPUTT

After an accident, the nurse had pierced his vein
And joined it by a curving plastic tube
To a bag suspended from a pole.
And I, a boy, was told to watch
That he did not move, frightened by a dream
Or goaded on by pain, and jerk his arm away.
He whispered hoarsely, "Weeds will not be killed,"
Again and yet again until the nurse
Had summoned me away, and now, old as he was then,
I am convinced that man is still alive.

< 39 >

INSULTING THE STARS

People see insults in nuances of manner and expression, more subtle that than an early morning mist. Was there perhaps a note of sarcasm in a soldier's voice, when he replied to his superior? Did he sound reluctant? Or too eager? We not only find abuse almost everywhere, but we remember it for decades, centuries, and even millennia. Human pride is so delicate, and requires such intense protection, that, at least since Paris eloped with Helen, people have gone to war over slights. We care more about pride than about food, shelter, and life itself.

Such fragility is shared by human beings alone, for one cannot, after all, insult the stars.

< 40 >

PSALM

The melancholy in the eyes of animals, of a squirrel who
    turns his head and looks at you a moment before
    scampering up a tree.
The melancholy of old shoes, old gloves, old walking sticks,
    all things a man has touched for many years.
A child begins to realize that people die, himself, his mother
    and father, all who live and all who are not yet born.
His eyes are wide, as if he were gazing at a ring of lights,
On a Ferris wheel, at some mysterious hour when he is
    usually asleep.
The melancholy of a city square at evening when vendors
    take in their stalls and pigeons circle toward rooftops
    for the night.
The girls walk back and forth, sadder than they realize,
    more beautiful than they can ever know.

< 41 >

THE MOTH

This visitor,
Born of a white flame
Kindled by a star,
Lands on my table.

Her huge round eyes
That never close
Are fixed on me,
Yet she does not speak.

Perhaps she is asleep
And so am I.

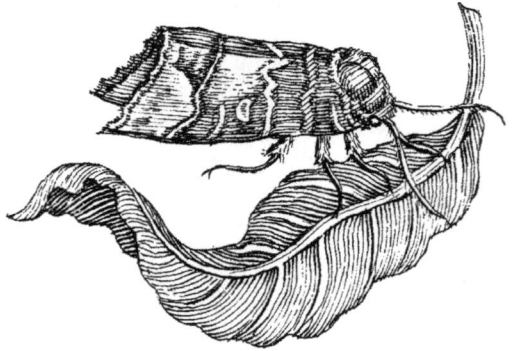

< 42 >

AFTER THE RAIN

Suddenly, the flicker
Of iridescent wings —
Two dragonflies in an embrace,
Now a single creature,
Rising, circling, hovering,
Above a pond.
This is the culmination of their lives
Which soon will end, but is the nuptial,
So synchronized and so precise,
Too perfect to be love?

< 43 >

THE DYING ANIMAL

When an animal dies, another of the same species may cling to the body, eat the body, or look bored. Bees expel dead bodies from the hive or, if that is impossible, embalm them in honey. Elephants "say" a ritualistic good-bye, and touch their dead before slowly walking away. Corvids often accept the death of a companion without much fuss, but they at times have "funerals," where scores of birds lament over the corpse of a deceased crow.

But it is a bit odd that people should investigate whether animals "comprehend death," as if human beings understood what it means to die. Is death a prelude to reincarnation? A portal to Heaven or Hell? Complete extinction? Union with all life? Or something else? All of these views can at times be comforting, yet people usually fear death, quite regardless of what they claim to believe.

In the natural world, killing seems a casual affair. Human beings, of course, kill on a massive scale, but most of us can only kill, if at all, by softening the impact of the deed through rituals such as drink or prayer. The strike of a spider, a heron, or a cat is swift and, seemingly, without inhibition or remorse. They pounce with a confidence that could indicate ignorance, indifference, or else profound knowledge. Could this be, perhaps, because animals cannot conceive of killing, since they are not aware of death? Could it be because they understand death well, far better than do human beings?

If animals envision the world not in terms of abstract concepts but sensuous images, the soul might appear as a unique scent, a rhythmic motion, or a tone of voice. Death would be the absence of these, though without that absolute finality that we find so severe. Perhaps the heron that snaps a fish thinks his meal lives on, as he one day will, in the form of currents in the pond.

< 44 >

ONE BEING

An owl seizes a mouse,
And, in an instant,
They become one being,
Knowing both triumph and terror.
The mouse, for the first time,
Glimpses the roofs of houses
And the tops of pines
As he dies, while the owl
Forgets him, passing
Across the moon.

< 45 >

FALL

I expect every summer to last
Forever, and then, suddenly, it is fall.

A single leaf is ripped from a branch.
Its sound is lost in the wind.

One cicada lies dead on the path.
Can another repeat his song?

This morning, the first snow of the year.
It is falling one snowflake at a time.

< 46 >

SO MUCH OF LIFE

So much of life is spent between one thing and another,
    waiting on the bus, for the laundry, or for work to start.
You sit in the lobby of a train station, leaning drowsily
    against the back of a wooden bench.
You wait to grow up, drive, graduate, and learn what death
    may bring.

It was morning and wheat sparkled in the sunlight
    where you strolled.
It was evening and the soft rain fell upon your shoulders,
    tiny droplets, barely visible at all.
You are all things that you have ever done, remembered,
    and forgotten as you sleep.

The day has passed like water, with countless changing
    shapes, between your fingers, underneath a stone.
For a moment you were water, then you were a gull,
    then light entering the chambers of a leaf.
For a moment you were dust, spreading through
    a country road, and rising as an auto hurried past.

What rhythm lingers in your footsteps and the way you
    turn your head or swing your arm?
You leave behind ideas, like socks left in the laundromat,
    like coins slipped from your pocket, lying beneath a chair,
And move to a tune learned in childhood, though the words
    have been forgotten long ago.

< 47 >

THE DESTINATION

I dream of flowers
not rooted in the earth,
which float through meadows,
Over streams, between trees,
Moving — like fish — in clusters:
Daisies, carnations, roses,
Flowers unknown to man,
Moved by neither wind
Nor the hand of any girl or boy.
Like me, they are searching for a home.

They pause before a field,
Circle, descending
Slowly, yet on touching ground
They instantly take root.
Following the scent, I come
And build my home.

< 48 >

SNOWMAN

The snowman, azure
At the height of day,
Then tinted crimson
By an evening cloud,
Takes on the blue or red
Of winter coats,
The black of branches, emerald of pines,
And all the many tones of human skin.

Suddenly in March, his flesh
Collapses to reveal
His soul made of water,
Streaked by sun.

< 49 >

THE VINE OF DREAMS

Snow falls into a hollow tree,
As seeds enter the earth.
I have seen flowers grow from rotting wood;
Let a vine of dreams extend
Out of a snowflake, as though from a seed,
With crystal leaves that twine
Around the branches of the mother tree
And throw rainbows on the snowy ground.

< 50 >

SNOW

The snowflakes, almost black
Against a lightless sky.
Crumbs of earth, splinters of darkness,
Till morning, but in the sun
A single flake catches a ray of light
To glimmer and to be lost
Inside the luminous multitude.
All afternoon, it snows.

Of shapes taken by flowing water,
All have vanished except for one.
Of sounds made by wind in the forest,
None are left but an ominous drone.
Through branches, diagonals of snow.
Snow fills the hollow tree,
While smoothing crevices in the bark.
Throughout the day, it snows.

Say that each snowflake is a person:
Touching the ground, they die.
They move in clusters, families or tribes.
A violent wind sweeps through them,
Lifts them, throws them against the hill,
And this is history. This is humankind.
I walk about in centuries of snow.

< 51 >

TREE OF KNOWLEDGE

The roots are nourished by the Milky Way.
Like the crack in an egg, one branch extends.
Around it, ice and talons of a crow.

Shaking the snow from his wings,
The crow ascends amid the nebulae.
His call is muffled by the stars.

< 52 >

THAT SNOWFLAKE

Chase the first snowflake
Of the year, with your eyes.
Say: "I am that snowflake."
Which snowflake? Where?
Even the wind is white.

< 53 >

STORIES

A VOICE, A PAIR OF HANDS

The green of meadows flashed so brightly on a summer day, it seemed as though the sky could barely hold it. A herd of mammoths ran across the plain, and hunters threw their spears. One animal, stuck several times, expired with a call, at once pathetic and triumphant. The men returned, many covered with blood. One, in excitement, exclaimed, "We are almost as great as a mammoth." But even he did not believe that, and his companions were silent. They had seen mammoths root up trees. If, occasionally, they killed one, that was a gift. The animal, in any case, was old and probably about to die.

One man said, "We are as fast as deer." The others laughed. A small, high voice unexpectedly joined in the merriment. Surprised, men turned their heads. They laughed more loudly, a bit angry, half embarrassed yet still pleased. Then they fell silent and hurried home.

The high laughter was from a little girl, dressed in coarse linen, hurrying through the grass. She would sometimes laugh suddenly, but then she would often become very still.

She was half a member of the tribe, yet like a wild animal.

Her father was a voice, her mother a pair of hands. That, at any rate, was about all she could remember of her parents. She had been found as an infant by a river, either lost or abandoned. Women had taken care of her in turn, and, to the surprise of many, she had survived. She followed the tribe, listening, doing chores, being fed, yet bound by no tie of kinship, a bit like the wolves that tagged along after the people in their wanderings, sometimes helping with the hunt and eating scraps.

Her mother and father must be, an elderly woman once told her, in a kingdom to the West. Yet the girl often thought she sensed the presence of her mother in a juniper tree, or in a vine heavy with grapes. Sometimes, it seemed, her father called, through a wind in the high trees. And sometimes, in the stillness of a snowfall, it seemed both of her parents were near.

That evening, an elder summoned fire from within a stone. The flame said, "I am hungry." Men piled on more logs.

At first, sparks rose in slow, leisurely curves. "See what I can do!" shouted the fire. A tower of flame erupted, and many sparks shot up suddenly, to either die or perhaps to kindle stars.

< 57 >

A single spark seemed, for a while, to remain in place. The small girl said, "Take me with you!" She ran up to the spark, but it then floated out of sight.

For a few weeks, there would be food. The light of the fire transformed the faces of the people, as it rose, declined and shifted about their eyes. The flame, and the strength of the mammoth, entered them.

While they were eating, nobody thought to speak. But, on finishing, the men and women looked about uncertainly. Over the past year, nine more people had been lost to plague, to accidents or wild beasts. There were now twenty in the tribe, and its survival was unsure. Yet it took boldness even to worry, and only now, after a fresh meal, did a few express their fears.

"Do animals respect us?" asked an elder. "We are not as strong as the bison nor as fleet as the ibex. We hunt, but not so well as the lion. We build, but not so well as the beaver. Where can we find friends?"

The tribe in the mountain was befriended by bears. These huge men and women looked like bears, their movements efficient though slightly awkward, their faces fierce though melancholy.

The tribe between the rivers was befriended by beavers. Their features were delicate yet robust. They built lovely houses with arched roofs.

The flame said, "I am sleepy," and crept into the stones. Men and women strolled into their cave. Soon, a warm breeze was crossing the plain. The girl who had chased a spark rested with her people a short distance into a cave, wrapped in the skin of a mammoth. Unable to sleep, she got up, moved to the opening of the cave and watched a herd of mammoths nibbling at distant trees. A single raindrop fell, catching the light of dying embers. She thought, "That could be me."

The sun went down, so quickly it was almost violent. Stars came out, far brighter and more plentiful than in any sky today. A dark cloud came, devouring the stars like a whale swallowing tiny fish. The mammoths were no longer visible, though the girl could still hear their footsteps. A few steps from her, everything faded into blackness.

Then, like the start of the universe, a firefly appeared. The girl stared a moment. It disappeared as suddenly as it had come.

But it was there again, a very short distance from her eyes. The girl reached out to touch the firefly, and it moved a bit further off. She rose

< 58 >

and began to follow. After taking a few steps, it was became so dark, the girl wondered if she had disappeared. "Is this what death is like?" she wondered. "Is this where the mammoth went? Are mother and father here?"

But then...

The firefly returned, rising and falling in a playful sort of way. "Follow me," it said, then vanished and reappeared. The girl followed it in the darkness, over hills, rocks and shallow streams. Soon, she had lost all thought of where, or even who, she was. There were strange sounds which she had never heard during the day. But she thought only of that tiny point of light.

At last, the firefly remained in place. The darkness said, "We can be friends." An entire swarm of fireflies hovered around the shoulders of the girl. Then, a human voice reached her. A party of three women and two men had ventured into the darkness in search of the girl. The features of an elderly man, their leader, became clearly visible, as he stepped from behind a tree and a firefly passed across his brow.

The sun appeared. One by one, a few leaves emerged from the darkness. The girl could see not only branches but the massive bodies of surrounding trees. And there, in a valley below, was the cave where her people stayed.

Soon the tribe of the girl adopted the firefly as totem. Men and women created lamps of stone. From a distance, their nightly camp itself looked like a swarm of fireflies. The tribe of the bear looked down from the mountain. A woman said, "These people are like thoughts of a god."

< 59 >

A NOOSE FOR THE SKY

Each day the King would climb the highest tower of his palace and gaze out the window at his lands. There was nothing — absolutely nothing — that did not belong to him. If he saw a chicken, he could have the chicken roasted. If he saw a tree, he could have the tree chopped down. If he saw a man, he could have the man killed. In short, he could do anything he pleased.

His Viceroy was bent like a banana. His Chancellor was tall and thin like a stick of celery. His General was round as a cabbage. And the King looked hungry!

The King wore his jewels the way a hedgehog wears its spikes. He was small, but he had a big voice. His glance made peasants tremble in their fields and (so the King believed) leaves tremble on the trees.

The king believed that even stones feared his power.

When there was something he wanted done, the King would ring for his Viceroy. The Viceroy would call the Chancellor. The Chancellor would whisper something to the General, and the General would shout at the soldiers. They would roast the chicken, chop down the tree, kill the man or shatter the stone.

One day, as the King was gazing out contentedly over the river, he looked up at the Sun. It was so bright that the King grimaced in pain and had to turn away his eyes.

The King was amazed. "Bring the Sun here! How dare it shine into my eyes!" he declared.

The King was about to turn his most terrifying glance on the Sun, the glance that made peasants tremble in their fields and leaves tremble on the trees. Looking up, he found the Sun was hiding behind a cloud.

The King called for his ministers. "Bring the Cloud here! How dare it hide my Sun!" he shouted.

"Your Majesty," answered the Viceroy, "forgive us, but we cannot fetch the Cloud. It belongs to the Sky."

"And does not the Sky fear my power?" asked the King. "Tell it I demand the Cloud."

"No, your Majesty," said the Chancellor, "The Sky is a great King like yourself, and will not obey."

At this, the King began to get angry.

< 60 >

"Then," said the King, "I must teach the Sky a lesson. Cut off its blue hair, then cover the hair with milk and sugar. Bring that to me in a bowl, and I will have it for breakfast."

"But, your Majesty," said the Viceroy, "that is impossible."

The King became angrier. "Then cut of the big blue toes of the Sky," he replied. "Grill them on a skewer and bring them to me. I will have them for lunch."

"But, your Majesty," said the Chancellor, "that is impossible."

At this, the King was very angry indeed. "Then cut off the blue ears of the Sky," he shouted. "Fry them, and bring them to me on a plate. I will have them for dinner."

"Please, your Majesty," said the General, "that is impossible. We can shoot arrows into the Sky or slash it with our swords, but the wounds just heal at once."

"What?" said the King, "Then the Sky, the Cloud, and the Sun must be imprisoned."

The ministers wanted to object, but they saw that the King had grown very angry.

"Tomorrow, the Sky, the Cloud, and the Sun will be captured,"they replied together.

The Viceroy confided with the Chancellor, then the Chancellor whispered something to the General. And that night, as the King was sleeping, the soldiers placed bars on all of the windows.

When the King woke, he demanded that his ministers show him the imprisoned Sky, the Cloud, and the Sun.

"As you can see, they are behind bars," the Viceroy replied.

The King nodded and said, "You have done well."

For a long time, the ministers lived in fear. "Any day," they thought, "the King will step outside of his palace and realize what we have done."

But the King never seemed to think of leaving. He seemed to have forgotten that the palace had an outside at all.

The Viceroy whispered to the Chancellor, then the Chancellor shouted at the General. So that the King might not stray out of the palace by accident, the General ordered the palace extended.

Soldiers built a roof over the courtyard. They added a corridor to the lodge. The towers grew ever higher.

< 61 >

Strangers came from as far as Rome, Thebes, and Samarkand to marvel at the size of the palace. Occasionally somebody would be chopped down like a tree or roasted like a chicken, but they kept right on coming.

Then, one day, the King looked out from between the bars and, once again, the Sun shone in his eyes.

He gazed a second time and, once again, the Sun was hiding behind a Cloud. "Even in prison, they still defy me!" shouted the King.

He called for his ministers, and proclaimed, "The Sky, the Cloud, and the Sun have been imprisoned a long time, but they have learned nothing at all. They cannot be reformed, so they will have to be hanged. In an hour, you must set up three ropes on the oak beside the river. I will watch the execution of the Sky."

The ministers bowed in unison and promised to do as they were told. The Viceroy gestured to the Chancellor, then the Chancellor shook his finger at the General. Soon the soldiers were tying the heaviest ropes that could be found to the oak beside the river. Then everyone formed a circle and stood waiting for the King.

As the King rode through the palace door, he looked up and shouted, "The Sky has escaped! The Cloud has escaped! The Sun has escaped!"

"Bring them back at once!" screamed the King!

"The Sky has escaped!" shouted the viceroy, and he ran into the woods.

"The Cloud has escaped!" shouted the chancellor, and he ran into the woods.

"The Sun has escaped!" shouted the General, and he ran into the woods.

The soldiers scattered in all directions.

Now completely alone, the King glared straight at the Sun, with the glance that made peasants tremble in their fields and leaves tremble on the trees. He was blinded; he fell from his horse and lay senseless on the ground.

When they saw the King on the grass, the ministers approached slowly. Then the soldiers gently carried the King back into his palace

< 62 >

and placed him upon the throne. They covered all of the windows with thick blankets, so that no light could get in.

The King woke up, and it seemed as if nothing had happened.

He looked fondly at the golden knives, ivory birds, jeweled cups, and silver plates, all glittering in the candlelight.

Slowly, the King began to remember about the Sky, the Sun, and the Cloud. He rang for his ministers, and demanded to know what they had done.

"As you can see, they have been killed," the Viceroy said. He pointed to the windows, now completely black.

"We attacked the Sky," the Chancellor explained, "but the Sun got in the way. We shot at the Sun with arrows and slashed at it with swords. But, when it was almost captured, the Cloud came and hurled lightning bolts at us."

"After battling for many hours," the General concluded, "we realized that we could not capture our enemies alive. We threw our spears into their hearts."

"You are good ministers," said the King. "You have done well."

"Thank you, your Majesty," the ministers replied together.

Having vanquished even the Sky, the King felt no need to leave his palace any more. When he looked out of the windows, he could see nothing at all. And so, in the surrounding Kingdom, the King ordered no more chickens to be roasted, no more trees to be cut down, no more men to be killed and no more stones to be broken apart.

A little girl came to pick flowers by the river. Some boys made the ropes hanging from the oak into a swing. A crane built a nest over the tower. It rained. It snowed. The Sun came out, then hid behind a cloud. Finally, the walls of the palace were completely covered with vines and shrubs.

People thought it was a mountain. Only a few old men and women remembered having heard of the King or his palace.

And nobody at all knew what happened to them. Perhaps the King finally realized his foolishness and went away. Or perhaps he and his ministers are there still.

< 63 >

GRANDMOTHER AND DEATH

Grandmother's speech was clear yet incoherent, like that of somebody in full possession of her mental powers yet dreaming. She would forget who was dead and who was alive. The memories of her early childhood in Russia seemed more vivid to her than the events of the last ten years. Each disconnected phrase was uttered with an intonation so authoritative that it seemed to hold a profound truth. If she said, "The bear is coming," I would look around the apartment for a bear.

Everyone expected her to die very soon. They had for years. Yet she lived on. She only sank more deeply into a dream, a timelessness which could be a premonition of eternity.

Sometimes I thought she could live forever. I would sit at her bedside recounting my childhood memories, uncertain if I were speaking to her or to myself. Occasionally her eyes would focus on me, though such moments became increasingly rare.

Finally, she ceased to acknowledge my name. But even then, I could not believe the word never reached her. Perhaps, in the landscape of her mind, my name became a bird flying briefly across the sky. I hope that it was a vivid one. Perhaps, even if unnoticed, it made the sunlight on the river seem brighter and the fields seem richer. Who knows?

One afternoon I spoke to her of a cottage where we had spent the summer thirty years ago. I had been a small child then, while she already had long, grey hair. At my words grandmother rose slightly and turned in my direction, her eyes unfocused but intense, like those of a statue from the days of the pharaohs.

Her gaze, though not directed at me, seemed to take me in. This time perhaps I was an isolated tree in a field of tall grass. A tree before that summer cottage? Or even the tree above her house in the Russian village where she grew up?

I stood nearly motionless. She sank back into the chair and closed her eyes. "Nadya," I called. She did not respond. She was asleep. Yet sleep and waking, I imagine, were both nothing more than a change of scene in the dream-theater that her life had become.

I could sense the presence of Death. Not that the moment for him had necessarily come. He was probably not here on business. He may have just stopped in to warm himself from the chilly October wind.

< 64 >

He as standing mutely in the corner, looking around and rubbing his hands. In a while he would continue on his rounds.

I left both of them — my grandmother and Death — to converse in their secret way. A bit tired myself, I craved the sunshine and even the brisk, cold air.

As I walked down the musty corridor of the apartment, everything acquired a new intensity. I noticed stains upon the wall. I noticed a crack in a wooden table. Every accidental feature of the place had a heroic finality. It was like a building where some document that changed the world had been signed, a structure later consecrated as a historical monument and preserved unchanged by curators.

As I opened the door of the building, light flashed from the wing of a seagull. Wind shook a nearby tree, making the sun and shade play about my face. Shouts of children echoed from the façades of buildings. I thought how the passing of my grandmother would sever a final link with my own childhood. I had always been a bit of a child for her, but soon I would begin to grow old.

My senses heightened by an awareness of mortality, I perceived everything with unaccustomed sharpness. "Perhaps," I thought, "I am really dead." Random memories passed through my mind in rapid succession. The figure of my grandmother seemed to preside over these memories, her long white hair floating behind her.

Then, gradually, the mundane rhythm of everyday life began to reassert itself. Nothing remarkable, after all, had happened. The day merged back into the succession of other days, which were to be lost in the passing of decades. My recollection of the morning had already begun to fade.

An hour later I returned to find my grandmother, sunk back into a chair with her eyes closed. The steady breathing told me that she was still alive.

< 65 >

ISHMAEL

A large sycamore stood by a bench in a small park next to a busy thoroughfare. The local historian said it was well over 200 years old, though there was no record of its early growth. All sights and sounds converged amid its branches to produce a sensuous sort of intuition. A vision shivered through leaves, branches, stem and roots, filling the smallest crevice. If a bird landed on a branch, or a gust of wind rattled by, the sycamore was aware. The sycamore knew when a person was passing by. It knew if the person was a man or a woman. The tree could even tell if the person was young or old, elated or depressed.

Every afternoon a man named Ishmael sat on the bench under the tree. He watched children play or robins hop across the lawn. He listened to the wind in the leaves above him. After a day of work, he would usually remain about fifteen minutes, long enough to calm his nerves. As he approached retirement age, however, his duties at the office became increasingly ceremonial. He would leave early and spend longer periods on the bench beneath the sycamore.

Even as a child, he had sometimes played at being a tree. He had gone into the yard, closed his eyes, spread his arms and stretched out his fingers. Then he had felt the wind and swayed softly back and forth. Often there had been a few moments of peace, not quite like anything he had ever known before. The thoughts of a test at school, an itch or a grumbling stomach had abruptly broken the mood. Ishmael would stop and stare in front of himself, amazed to remember who he really was.

In a world where nobody wishes to be ordinary yet everyone is, Ishmael was strangely blessed (or cursed). He had wished to be ordinary, yet could not. He did all of the ordinary things. He had a modest but dignified career as an electronics technician. He had suffered about his share, neither more nor less. He had married, though his wife was long dead and his children were grown. But, though he had never done anything very unusual, he seemed completely unlike anyone else. There was an almost unearthly steadiness in the rhythm of his footsteps.

< 66 >

After retirement, Ishmael would sometimes spend entire days in that place. He might read or exchange a few words with children. But often he would just watch and listen. His ears became so attuned to the sycamore, he could tell just by listening which boughs were moving in the wind. Sometimes he would find a leaf on the ground and know the precise place on a branch that it had come from.

Ishmael was small and fastidious. Alert though his features were, these now seemed almost hidden among the heavy lines of his face. Seated on his favorite bench, he seemed to blend into the scenery so completely that people hardly even noticed him. Neighbors never complained about his loitering.

A few young men, at that age when cynicism is confused with maturity, remarked that the old guy was about as lively as the tree beside him. One morning, after sleeping late, Ishmael approached the bench and found the sycamore had been cut down. The stem had already been cut into logs and hauled away, though many leafy branches were still scattered about the grass. A bright November sun gave the stump a nearly unnatural whiteness, like a meteor heated on a star.

After a moment of shock, Ishmael recovered his composure. He sat down on the bench as usual, yet soon he began to fidget. He decided to take a walk to calm himself. Though nothing else was changed, the shops and homes that Ishmael had passed a thousand times had lost their familiarity. Ishmael recognized everything, but all the buildings looked somehow different. The shopkeepers were friendly as usual, but now Ishmael thought he detected an excessive formality in their greetings. All of a sudden, he was a stranger. Ishmael wandered through the streets until he came to a wood. As he strolled along, the remaining daylight highlighted with particular clarity all of the intricate textures of bark, stone and fallen leaves. These objects seemed to shimmer, but this play of light and shadow was broken by heavy areas of dark green under the hemlock boughs. Otherwise everything, even the boulders, seemed about to float away. Ishmael strayed from the path.

As he went on, the nature of the woods started to change. Instead of being carefully trimmed, the trees became more gnarled and misshapen. The woods became darker. Ishmael found, however, that his movements took on a rhythm that rendered him almost indifferent to such sensations as weariness.

< 67 >

Though no path was visible ahead, the trees made way for Ishmael, like people in a crowd. Ahead he could hear the rustling of the sycamore under which he had spent so many afternoons. It seemed as if his body were a lute, vibrating with these gentle sounds. Then it was a single note, sailing above the ground. Then, slowly acquiring weight, it became a seed.

Reaching a slight clearing, Ishmael threw himself to the ground. He saw all of the blades of grass in front of him merge into a single cloud of green. He felt himself slowly rising. A soft, cool sensation surrounded him like fresh, clean sheets on a spring night.

Suddenly, he became aware of myriad tiny sounds. He heard squirrels hurrying through fallen leaves and even the beating wings of jays over his head. Ishmael was a tree, a sycamore. Other trees sent him messages of welcome through the wind.

Perhaps he had learned something in those childhood games. At any rate, he was not frightened to recognize the change. He simply whispered to himself, "At last." His thought spread like a cloud of mist about the wood. Though clear in detail, his life as a person now seemed remote. He understood the other trees better than he had ever understood fellow human beings. But many people whom he had known before, also transformed, were now beside him. Their minds seemed to join like branches in the forest canopy.

For a long time, his absence had gone unnoticed, much as his presence had before. A month later, at the request of the landlord, a locksmith opened the door to Ishmael's room. On entering they found everything meticulously arranged. The place was immaculate. The hole Ishmael had left in the world sealed up easily as water after a swimmer leaves a pond.

< 68 >

DOCTOR BONES

The watchman making his rounds in a Macy's needn't worry about spooks. If he hears a noise, he can safely assume it is either a burglar or an accident. The vast rooms contain rows of identical dresses, nails, boxes of tea. ... Everything is ordered and immaculate. There is no ancient life to be revived. Even during a stormy night, the merchandise will not seem to be inhabited by spirits. Nobody will say he has heard the mannequins speak.

Everything there exists as potential, neither more nor less. Objects in the sales racks wait for the buyer to animate them in her home. She will stain the tablecloth and crack the wooden bowl, like a goddess bringing these things to life.

But if there is a watchman in a thrift shop, he will be well advised to bring along a silver cross. Each shirt in the shop will have stretched and shrunk in a unique way. However often a jacket may have been cleaned, there will be smells in the fabric waiting to be revived. If an electric fan blows down a row of dresses, each will flutter in a different way, and move like people parading along a busy street.

Most people who visit a thrift store will do so for pragmatic reasons — to buy inexpensive clothing or household items, and run their fingers through piles of belts or sweaters. Others will come in search of a magic charm. Among the hats could be a hat that renders the wearer invisible. In the jewelry section could be an amulet that enables the wearer to change her shape.

The Brothers Grimm once wrote of a stick in a burlap bag that, on the command of the owner, would rise of its own accord and beat an enemy. They wrote of a table cloth that, if spread upon the ground, would instantly be covered with the most delicious foods. There is also said to be a knapsack which contain seven soldiers, always ready to do the owner's bidding. There are bones that sing and bottles that contain jinn.

That, at any rate, was the theory of Dr. Bones. As a young man he had approached problems in physics or chemistry with unusual zeal and enthusiasm. Even then, however, his initial elation at solving a problem had often given way to melancholy. He had longed for a world in which explanations would be impossible and unnecessary, where questions would not even have to be asked.

< 69 >

Accordingly, Dr. Bones spent over a year shuffling through various thrift stores and even a few town dumps. Every now and then he would spot an ax or a cloak that looked somehow uncanny. Trusting his intuition, he would purchase the object and bring it home. He would use, wear, or eat the thing in question, yet nothing miraculous would happen. Once removed from the environment of the thrift store, he would find the ax or cloak seemed to lose its magical aura. Slowly Dr. Bones went over the data and began to formulate a hypothesis.

"Some objects," he theorized, "are truly inanimate, while other objects merely pretend to be so." Many in the tales by the Brothers Grimm were said to have performed their feats during a period of comparative joy and innocence. These objects were trusting. They revealed their power to anyone who came along. The ones which have not been burned or shattered have now survived in an era of concentration camps and wars far bloodier than any previous conflicts. They realize how easy it is to be abused or destroyed.

So went the theory. One example the good Doctor used was the stick within a sack. According to Grimm, this cudgel would come out immediately on a command from the owner and beat an antagonist.

But, over the centuries, the stick — if it is still around — must surely have become more suspicious of people. It may, therefore, be expected to just stay in the bag, at least until it learns something about the owner and the antagonist. On sensing the presence of a human being, such an object may freeze like a doe in a headlight. This, however, does not mean it will not speak at all.

Accordingly, the task of Dr. Bones was to observe such objects when they did not suspect an intruder. This would not be easy, since the magic objects had centuries of experience to draw on. But, in his bold yet meticulous manner, Dr. Bones began to construct a plan by which the objects could be fooled. Such objects, he concluded, were most likely to converse at night in the Salvation Army Store. Due to the comparatively low marketability of the merchandise in such a shop, no night watchman had ever been assigned to remain on guard there. The magic objects, in consequence, would be relatively careless.

Dr. Bones quit his job at a university and dropped from public view. Under an assumed identity, he obtained work as a security guard. By faking a few attempted break-ins and cultivating useful contacts, Dr. Bones managed to have himself assigned to the store in question.

< 70 >

Entering the main room discreetly, Dr. Bones heard a voice: "Everything is friendly here," said a wooden bowl. "I'm glad to have come."

"You are welcome," said a candlestick. "I have remained on this shelf for many years. Dear friends have come and gone. It is cozy here, though I am sometimes frustrated by inactivity. I miss the time when a little girl lit me every evening and polished me every week."

"Once a mother used me almost daily to mix dough for bread," replied the bowl.

"That was perhaps a hundred years ago. I was happy then. But there is probably no human being alive today as gentle as that young woman was. These are bitter times...."

At this point Dr. Bones raised his head ever so slightly, hoping to hear better. But, abruptly, the conversation stopped. There was, in fact, a silence more intense than any the good Doctor had ever known before, as if he were a cosmonaut who had just landed on some lifeless, frozen planet.

For a moment even the faintest currents in the air had ceased. The water in a nearby stream no longer flowed. Dr. Bones thought the end of the world was at hand. Then suddenly an old burlap bag across the room stood up on its own accord. Out popped a rough, oaken cudgel. The stick flew straight across the room and hit Dr. Bones on the shoulder, sending him to the floor. The good Doctor rolled over and tried to rise, but a few more sharp blows sent him down again. He somehow scrambled to the store window and jumped through. Then he ran away through the empty streets, aching from the bruises but pleased.

< 71 >

CHICAGO

The comradeship among boys during early adolescence is so intense it seems destined to last forever. I went everywhere with my friends (everywhere was school, the pizza parlor, our homes, and a few parks). By himself, no one of us ever felt complete.

But what created this bond? We didn't talk much about our families, since the subject reminded us that we were kids. We didn't talk much about girls, since we hardly dared to think about them. We talked about class, rumors, baseball and even world affairs, all things we didn't usually care too much about. But that didn't matter, because our friendships were not based on talk. They had amazingly little basis, yet they also required little. Now, when I meet with friends, we must have something to talk about or to do. Back then we could simply luxuriate in the presence of one another.

Yet the friendships proved as ephemeral as they were intense. During the first year of college, the old high school friends and I did remain sporadically in touch, though our few meetings were marked by awkward silences. My life was being filled with all the things that our early friendships had excluded: romance, responsibilities, serious failures, successes, and long-term plans. The lives of my friends had also changed, and adulthood seemed like a betrayal of our bond. Within a few years, I had not only lost touch with these old friends but forgotten them entirely.

Now, having recently entered middle age, I am sometimes abashed to find myself sitting here at a desk — very happily married, writing, teaching, and generally content, yet unsure of how all this came about. I sometimes feel as though I were without a past, as though I had simply appeared here by magic, possessions, friends, and all.

I still have no desire to meet my adolescent buddies once again. Even if we were to begin new friendships, we still could not resurrect the old ones. But, since I know how easily they can fade, I value memories more. And, superficial though they proved to be, the early friendships are still, in many ways, the most intense relationships with other males that I have known and the model for all that came afterwards.

And now, I search my mind for some epiphany, some special afternoon or moment to fix those early friendships in my memory. The

< 72 >

days seem to merge together, and it is hard to pick out any one. But, perhaps at a certain age, when barely emerging from the timelessness of childhood, it is not the special days but the typical ones that are important. Ours always seemed close to both menace and euphoria, threats and promises that never were fulfilled.

Nothing could ever be duller than the big city, with its interminable blocks of grey and brown, broken only by garish neon signs. The romance of danger, however, made the monotony endurable, at least for young boys. Danger surrounded us like a luxuriant tropical garden with snakes of a hundred feet, flowers large as a man, leopards of blue and green.

Our neighborhood was full of clandestine events. A limousine would drive up to an abandoned gas station at night and receive admittance. A restaurant had a dark room in the back, which would seemingly go almost unused. There were rumors of severed heads found in garbage cans, and of human beings fed to rats. Such tantalizing esoteric knowledge, shared by boys who lived there, made us, we imagined, superior to other people.

It united us. "Yes, we know" — we signaled this to one another with slightly conspiratorial glances.

We sat together one evening, three of us, sprawled across the room, saying very little, but feeling the presence of one another, exulting in our secret knowledge. Each boy had a facade of toughness, barely enough to fool himself, let alone the other boys and certainly not the world. There was Fred, now collapsed like a marionette over the sofa, elbows, knees and hands pointing in all directions. And there was Warren, often the class clown, his normally animated features staring limply into space. I was the third, so dreamy I had once walked through a locked door made of glass.

Then, suddenly, I realized with excitement and alarm that it was after midnight. "Till tomorrow." "Till tomorrow." And I was alone on the street.

I was afraid of the darkness, the street lights, gangs, zombies and many other things. And the fear made me feel important. I walked faster, slipping into a sort of nervous euphoria.

Suddenly, there was a shot. "Where?" I said to myself. But the street was more silent than before. What was I to do? Run? Scream?

< 73 >

I decided to simply walk on. And, in a moment, I was no longer sure if I had really heard or only imagined the shot. I quickened my pace. Discreetly, for I did not wish my fear to show.

A shadowy figure appeared at the end of the street. As each of us approached the other and realized there was no criminal intent, our momentary nervousness changed to comradeship. We still, however, did not dare acknowledge this and say "hello." He lowered his face in passing, and I did the same.

Then a headlight, appearing suddenly, made me wince. A single car rattled by.

Another shot rang out! The direction was elusive as with the first. Looking around, I felt a slight dizziness, but there was nothing unusual to be seen.

In a while, I was safe at home, gazing out my window at the starlight diffused through smog. The haze was broken by street lights and an occasional lighted window. Then I remembered those two shots. I thought of my two friends, possibly dead yet probably long asleep. And I wondered who, among the few people in the city that I knew and the vast number I did not, might now be gone.

Many decades later, I still wonder about that now and then. Danger has long since lost its romance for me. My behavior then seems far closer to being moved by thoughtlessness than by love or courage, yet the fact is that I did routinely risk a great deal simply to be around my friends.

Yet now, looking out the window of my apartment, it is almost as if I had just finished that long walk home? Where, I wonder, is Fred? And where is Warren? Have they been killed? Or are they nestled in their beds?

And where, for that matter, is the boy I used to be?

< 74 >

ZEMYNE AND THE PEASANT

Loosely adapted from a Lithuanian legend

Zemyne is a snake with a single eye. Whoever she bites will die immediately. She may only be seen in summer, and then only at either noon or midnight. The blood of Zemyne is black, but it can cure every illness. Whoever bathes in the black blood of Zemyne is protected against all magic.

God has granted Zemyne dominion in the realm beneath the ground. The metals belong to her. "If I had two eyes instead of one," Zemyne once said, "I would kill enough people to cover the walls of my home with their skulls."

Zemyne was once a lovely young girl, who refused the advances of a wicked magician. Upon his curse, she assumed her present form. Whoever wishes to rescue her must beat her until her skin falls off. Then, he must burn the skin immediately.

A young peasant habitually killed all snakes that he found in the garden, forest and field. One day he was cutting grass in a meadow, when he suddenly heard a loud hiss. He became aware of a movement in the grass behind him. Looking around, he recognized Zemyne by her eye.

For a moment, he was transfixed by her reptilian gaze, intent yet without emotion. On second glance, he thought he discerned a melancholy. "That sadness," he thought, "must be the maiden."

To kill Zemyne would have given the peasant great power, but he had dreamed of rescuing the maiden. Seeing his chance, the peasant pinned the head of Zemyne firmly against the earth with the blade of his sickle. Then he grabbed a knotted branch with his free hand and pounded the snake furiously, until the skin of Zemyne broke open. All of a sudden, a beautiful maiden was standing before him. Beside her, in place of the snake's skin, sparkled a many-colored dress, made of silver, gold, and all the precious stones beneath the ground.

The maiden immediately reached for the dress, but the peasant was faster. He grabbed the garment, placed it beneath his arm and led the maiden to his home. There he gave her new garments and food. She sat across from him on a wooden bench, and smiled charmingly.

"Who are you?" asked the peasant.

< 75 >

The maiden did not answer.

"Where are you from?" he continued.

Again, she did not reply.

"Can you understand me?" he pleaded.

Still, she remained silent. Overwhelmed by her beauty and her mystery, the peasant leaned closer.

"Will you marry me?" he entreated.

"Yes," the maiden said.

The maiden's dress was so beautiful that the peasant could not bear to burn is it. Instead, he hid it in the woods.

And so, the two young people lived happily together for many years. Everything the wife planted — herbs, vegetables, and flowers — grew luxuriously. Neither deer, hares, nor rabbits would touch her crops. The house prospered so well that a few villagers whispered of witchcraft. But even they, in the end, were charmed by the recent bride.

While her garden aroused envy, Zemyne proved awkward in feminine arts such as embroidery. People found her clumsiness endearing. For women of the village, she proved a humble and willing pupil.

Zemyne went about her daily chores cheerfully, yet with a certain detachment. Her husband sometimes asked, "Do you love me?" She would reply without the slightest hesitation, "Yes." None could doubt her sincerity, yet the love did not seem like that of ordinary mortals. It was not domestic or even fully human. The passion appeared closer to the love that, philosophers say, moves the moon and stars.

Within a year, Zemyne gave birth to twins, a girl and a boy. Nearly every year brought another child, and soon the house was filled with the sounds of work and play.

As to her past, the wife claimed to remember nothing. She said this with a simplicity which seemed to render doubt or argument impossible. Yet often, when planting, she held the earth with such fondness that her husband felt a twinge of jealousy.

One day the wife glanced into the hollow of a tree, to see something glimmer in the depths. Reaching down, she found the many-colored dress. She put it on, changed immediately back into a snake, then greeted her husband with a poisonous kiss, and he joined her in the realm beneath the ground.

< 76 >

THE RAVEN AND THE SUN
(A LOOSE RETELLING
OF A HAIDA INDIAN MYTH)

Nine ravens are at play beside a hilly coast in the Outer Hebrides, beating their wings and gliding, diving and flipping over in the air. One spread his wings and does cartwheels in the breeze, then folds his wings and shoots down toward the ground, stops and hovers. The ravens are talking to one another, to the hills, to God.

But ravens do not speak, for they are a language. Nor dance, for they are dance.

"Kwarrrrrrrkk!"

They play with time, as a cat plays with a ball of yarn. One raven spreads her wings and somersaults, to land in air upon her back, and then flies upside down. Not only do ravens move back in time but also sideways, up, and down in time. They do somersaults in time.

"What time is it?" cries one raven. "What is time?" another raven responds.

The spirits of animals long dead come to watch. There is a cave bear, a mammoth, an Irish elk.

People also come. A lone motorist has stopped his car, and looks up at the sky. A shepherd looks up from a nearby hill. Perhaps the ravens are even talking to human beings, for they know full well that they are being watched. The long feathers of their outstretched wings are fingers of a hand, which point at one another, or even at a man or woman below.

One raven, with long whiskers, asks, "If the sun were a coin, what might you buy with it?" Another, with smooth feathers glinting, now purple and now green, laughs.

A third raven appears, carrying in its claws something flexible and long. It is the afterbirth of a lamb. It is a good meal. She drops it, catches it, and reascends, then carries it to a branch and starts to eat.

After a nibble, she calls out to the long-whiskered raven, "You stole the sun."

"I did not steal it! I could not, for it was mine!" he replies.

The ravens circle around him, as the ghost of the bear stands , and the ghost of the elk raises his head. The motorist raises his head half though the window, and the shepherd sits down. Sun-stealer, the raven with great whiskers, begins his story:

< 77 >

There was only darkness. God had painted the mountains and rivers the world with black pigment on a black board. Black trees grew from the dark soil. Men cut them down, to build black homes. Nobody who has not seen it can imagine such darkness, but I remember it very well. It was not the darkness of ignorance, but the darkness of knowledge. This darkness was alive as the world beneath the waves. The darkness divided, folded, flowed and grew, to make trees and villages. Farmers plucked fruits of darkness from black trees. They ate the darkness at mealtimes, and drank the wine of darkness in their pubs. Above them, we ravens glided on dark currents among the mountains.

It all seemed very natural, as this world seems natural to us now. Nobody thought it odd or strange, nor felt any need to see the world. It was, they thought, enough simply to know.

But I did not think so. Not me. Somewhere, I knew, there was a sun and a moon. We did not need them then, yet I knew they must be beautiful.

I felt the light, which I could not see. It was a trembling in the wind through my feathers, and extra warmth that reached me through the sky. I knew it the way human scientists know of forces and of particles that they can barely think and do not hope to see.

"Krrrrrronnnka!" "Where is the light?" I called.

As the wind shook me, I flew up to a cedar tree, where I became a needle on a twig. The cool wind closed around me, then the wind turned into rain.

The breeze shook me again. I let go, and drifted downward, turning as I fell.

On the bank was the daughter of a chief, and I, though there was no light to see, knew that she was beautiful. She cupped her hands to drink, and I floated into them.

Her hands were gentle as moss. Then she became a ridge of mountains, and the water in her hand became a lake. Her eyes became clouds and her mouth became a vast grotto. Her breath flowed east, while the water slowly flowed west, and I drifted along into a cavernous opening that echoed calls of gulls outside.

Then, suddenly, the water disappeared, and I was falling, endlessly falling.... I knew that soon I would be born.

< 78 >

And there I was, a child, a human child, sitting on the floor in the dwelling of the chief. He lived in an apartment in some big city, though I do not know if it was Manhattan or Moscow, Victoria, Tokyo, or Rome. "Seth," said the king's daughter, "...let his name be Seth, after the third son of Adam." "Yelth!" I called, and that became my name.

Outside, I could see pillars of steel and glass, that went down almost endlessly, and between them was the sky. In the distance below, I could hear a crashing like trees in a hurricane.

My grandfather looked at me. Dressed as befitting a chief, he wore a black suit, a white shirt, and a red tie. He owned a factory, one that made planets and stars. His face was heavily lined, weary for he had lived since the start of time.

"I want a rattle," I said, and my mother brought a rattle, carved of wood with a raven head. I shook it, so the beak clattered, and there was thunder outside, then rain.

"I want the sun," I said.

"Oh, no!" laughed the chief, who I had thought never laughed. "Nobody may touch the sun. It is too precious, too hot, too fragile. I keep the sun in a box in my basement, and the box is held by iron chains. Inside the box is another box, and inside it another.... It will stay there, stored securely, until the end of time."

"I want the sun," I said.

"Oh, no!" sighed the chief, who I had thought never sighed. Then he became silent and thoughtful.

"I want the sun," I said.

The chief remained silent for several minutes. At last, he said softly, "I too would like to see the sun."

He gestured to his servants, who left, to return a bit later with a black box. They placed it before me, then bowed slightly and retreated to the wall. The chief approached, and, at his touch, the sides of the box fell, to reveal another box, a red box. There were boxes with boxes, boxes of many colors — green, purple, orange, silver, blue.... Then finally, when all had fallen away, I saw the sun.

Until then, there had been no time, but suddenly it was early morning. This was the birth of death.

Suddenly, I was no longer a human being. I was a raven once more. I jumped up, grabbed the sun, and flew away.

< 79 >

The chief and his daughter watched me from a window, showing neither anger nor surprise.

I saw the cedar tree, where once I had been a needle, and the river where I had once floated away. I saw forests that were endless as the sky, and rivers that, like bands, held mountains and plains in place. I saw bears and seals flocking by huge blocks of ice.

And yet, the more I saw, the less I seemed to know. I felt frightened, as I had never been before. Light glinted on every needle in the cedar forest.

The chief, now an eagle, flew behind me, and reached for the ball of light. He lunged at me with his talons, and I turned and slipped away, as the ball poured across the sky and broke into many pieces.

The sun spread less like light than like water, cascading over mountains, and leaping among clouds. It filled enormous basins, until I could hardly see, but the darkness did not return.

Next thing I remember, I was perched, still in raven form, in a cedar tree. Looking up, I saw for the first time the moon and stars.

Sun-stealer circled the field one more time, and then flew off to the West, as the other ravens followed. The mammoth and elk vanished. The shepherd turned his flock towards home, and the motorist drove on.

< 80 >

ACKNOWLEDGMENTS

Previous versions of some poems in this volume have appeared in the collections *Rheinland Market* and *I Am That Snowflake*. Versions have also appeared in the journals *Poesie Europe, Parabola, Greenprints, Archae, Sacred Path, Archae, The Nature in Legend and Story Newsletter,* and *Westchester Review*. All of the poems here appear in their current versions for the first time.

Most of the illustrations for this book have been taken from the book series Dover Pictorial Archives. Some of them the illustrations have been digitally modified, modestly but enough to match them with the format of this book. The photographs, which accompany the poems "Fall," and "That Snowflake" are by W. A. Bentley. The crow wheels on the cover and facing the title-page are the work of artist Tom Fitzpatrick.

The story that gives this book its title requires a few words of explanation. Native Americans are now uneasy about having people who are not Indians retell their stories. Some of them see it is a form of cultural appropriation. But, then, I am not pretending to be, or trying to be, an Indian. As any folklorist knows, stories can transcend their cultural traditions. The tale of "Cinderella," for example, appears to have originated in ancient Egypt, but the first complete versions are from early medieval China. It has been recorded from oral traditions in over 900 versions, including several Native American ones. Even the story of the raven and the sun may not necessarily be a purely Native American one, since it has resemblances to the story of Christ, called "the light of the world," retold in an Indian cultural context. The raven might be an equivalent of Jesus; the Chief, of God the Father; and his daughter, of Mary. One need not be Native American — nor, for that matter, Christian — to find inspiration in the story.

< 81 >

ABOUT THIS BOOK

The type used in this book is Aldine, designed by Hermann Zapf to complement his earlier type family Palatino. Aldine emulates the typefaces of Aldus Manutius, the great Renaissance printer, publisher and humanist. Those early Italian type designs were themselves inspired by the initials in Roman stone carvings. Titles for this book are in Arrus, a typeface designed by Richard Lipton in 1991, based on his own calligraphic alphabets.

< 82 >